Intermediate Unit 5
Maintaining Financial Records and Preparing Accounts

Fourth edition April 2006

ISBN 0 7517 2621 4 (Previous edition 0 7517 2364 9)

British Library Cataloguing-in-Publication Data

A catalogue record for this book is available from the British Library

Published by

BPP Professional Education, Aldine House, Aldine Place, London W12 8AW

www.bpp.com

Printed in Great Britain by Ashford Colour Press

All our rights reserved. No part of this publication may be reproduced, stored in a retrieval system or transmitted, in any form or by any means, electronic, mechanical, photocopying, recording or otherwise, without the prior written permission of BPP Professional Education.

©
BPP Professional Education
2006

Welcome to BPP's AAT **Passcards.**

- They **save you time**. Important topics are summarised for you.
- They incorporate **diagrams** to kick start your memory.
- They follow the overall **structure** of the BPP Course Companions, but BPP's AAT **Passcards** are not just a condensed book. Each card has been separately designed for clear presentation. Topics are self contained and can be grasped visually.
- AAT **Passcards** are **just the right size** for pockets, briefcases and bags.
- AAT **Passcards focus on the assessment** you will be facing.
- AAT **Passcards focus on the essential points** that you need to know in the workplace, or when completing your skills test or exam.

Run through the complete set of **Passcards** as often as you can during your final revision period. The day before the exam, try to go through the **Passcards** again! You will then be well on your way to completing your exam successfully.

Good luck!

		Page
1	Revision of accounting systems and double entry bookkeeping	1
2	From ledger accounts to the trial balance	9
3	Introduction to financial statements	15
4	Accounting concepts and standards	23
5	Capital expenditure, depreciation and disposals	27
6	Final accounts and the accounting system	39
7	Accruals, prepayments and bad/doubtful debts	47

		Page
8	Stock	55
9	The extended trial balance	63
10	Sole traders	67
11	Partnerships	73
12	Incomplete records	85

1: Revision of accounting systems and double entry bookkeeping

Topic List

Recording and summarising

Assets and liabilities

Double entry

Posting from day books

This chapter revises double entry. You should be familiar with these topics, either from your Foundation studies, or from a bookkeeping course.

| Recording and summarising | Assets and liabilities | Double entry | Posting from day books |

Alert. This material should be very familiar to you.

Books of original entry

Source documents: sources of data recorded by business

Invoice: request for payment

Credit note: seller cancels part or all of an invoice

Books of original entry record **all** documented transactions

Sales day book: list of invoices sent to customers each day. (Remember the **sales returns day book.**)

Purchase day book: record of invoices received from suppliers. (Remember the **purchases returns day book** also.)

Cash book: cumulative record of monies received and paid out via the bank account.

Petty cash book: records cash received and paid out from the cash float.

Journal: records double entries not arising from the other books of original entry.

Main ledger

This summarises the financial transactions of the business. It details all assets, liabilities, income and expenditure. It records all capital and revenue transactions.

Discounts

Discounts: reduction in price of goods below that normally charged

Trade discount: reduction in the amount demanded from a customer

Cash discount: optional reduction in amount payable

| Recording and summarising | Assets and liabilities | Double entry | Posting from day books |

Assets

An item of value which a business owns or has the use of

Eg:

- Land and buildings
- Vehicles
- Stocks
- Cash

A **debtor** is an asset. A debtor is a person who owes money to the business.

Liabilities

Something which is owed to someone else

Eg:

- Bank loan/overdraft
- Amounts owed to trade creditors (suppliers)
- Tax

A **creditor** is a liability. A creditor is a person to whom money is owed by the business.

Fixed asset: an asset acquired for use within the business over more than one accounting period

Current assets: items owned by the business with the intention of turning them into cash

Cash is used to buy goods which are sold. Sales on credit create debtors, but eventually cash is earned from the sales. Some of the cash will then be used to replenish stocks.

Current liabilities: debts which must be settled within one year

Long-term liabilities: debts which are not payable within one year

The cash cycle

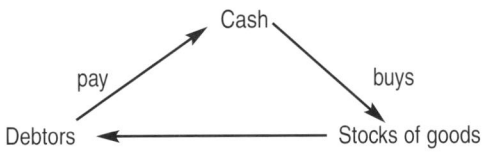

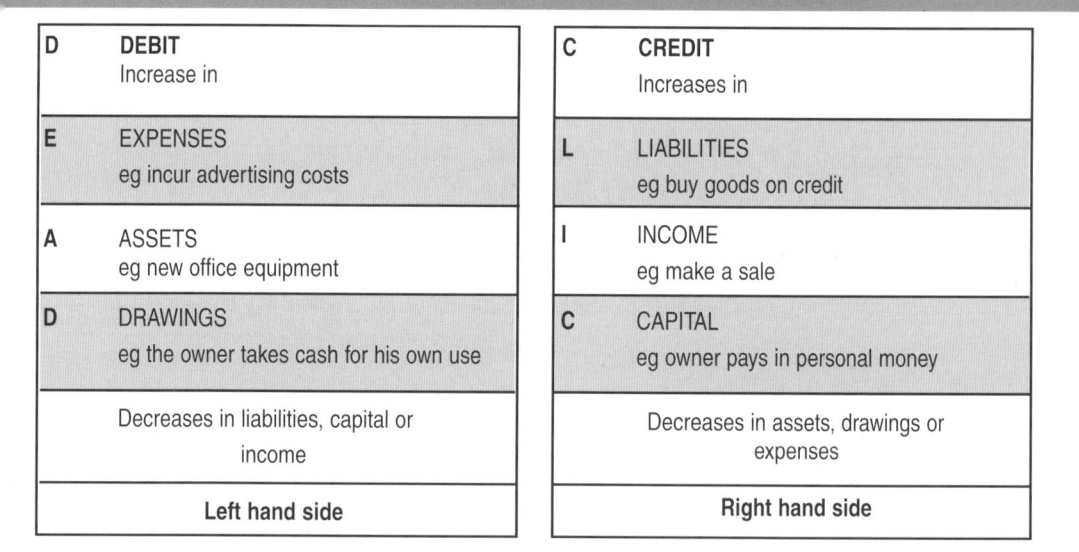

| Recording and summarising | Assets and liabilities | **Double entry** | Posting from day books |

D	**DEBIT** Increase in	**C**	**CREDIT** Increases in
E	EXPENSES eg incur advertising costs	**L**	LIABILITIES eg buy goods on credit
A	ASSETS eg new office equipment	**I**	INCOME eg make a sale
D	DRAWINGS eg the owner takes cash for his own use	**C**	CAPITAL eg owner pays in personal money
	Decreases in liabilities, capital or income		Decreases in assets, drawings or expenses
	Left hand side		**Right hand side**

Every transaction has a debit and a credit.

If a business buys goods for resale with cash then:

DEBIT   Purchases
CREDIT   Cash

Cash sales result in:

DEBIT   Cash
CREDIT   Sales

Total debits = Total credits

Accounting equation

Assets = Liabilities + Capital

Profit = Income - Expenditure

| Recording and summarising | Assets and liabilities | Double entry | **Posting from day books** |

The totals in the **sales day book** and the **purchase day book** are posted to the **sales ledger control** account and the **purchase ledger control account** respectively.

The **sales ledger** and **purchase ledger** record individual accounts. They are **memorandum** only, not part of the double entry.

Debit	Sales ledger control account
Credit	Sales
Debit	Purchases
Credit	Purchase ledger control account

2: From ledger accounts to the trial balance

Topic List

Sales and purchase ledgers

Control accounts

VAT

Errors

Trial balance

This chapter again covers ground which you should be familiar with. It takes you as far as the trial balance. You'll then be in a position to cover topics leading up to the extended trial balance and final accounts.

| Sales and purchase ledgers | Control accounts | VAT | Errors | Trial balance |

The main ledger contains **impersonal accounts**. The impersonal accounts relate to types of income, expense, asset and liability.

Personal accounts relate to the individual who is paid or from whom money is received. Personal accounts do **not** form part of the double entry. They are **memorandum** accounts.

Sales ledger

The **sales ledger** is a record of each of the business's customers.

The sales ledger allows the business to keep track of **who** owes it money and **how much** they owe.

The sales ledger:

- Shows customer **balances** and aids **queries**
- Allows the compilation of monthly **statements**
- Shows where an account is in relation to its **credit limit**
- Allows payments to be **matched** to invoices

Purchase ledger

The **purchase ledger** is made up of personal supplier accounts.

The purchase ledger allows the business to keep a track of **how much** it owes each **supplier** at any one time.

| Sales and purchase ledgers | **Control accounts** | VAT | Errors | Trial balance |

Control accounts

A **control account** is the grand total of similar items (usually debtors or creditors) recorded in the main ledger.

The main control accounts are:

- **Sales ledger control account**
- **Purchase ledger control account**

The control account value should agree with the **total of the individual balances**.

Other control accounts can be used for:

- **Stocks**
- **Wages and salaries**
- **VAT**

| Sales and purchase ledgers | Control accounts | **VAT** | Errors | Trial balance |

Accounting for VAT

VAT is a tax on the sale of goods and services. Standard rate of VAT is 17.5%. **Gross price = Net price + VAT**.

Output VAT

VAT on goods or services sold.

DEBIT	Cash (or debtors) £1,175	
CREDIT	Sales	£1,000
CREDIT	VAT account	£175

Input VAT

VAT on goods or services purchased.

DEBIT	Purchases	£800
DEBIT	VAT account	£140
CREDIT	Trade creditors	£940

Each quarter the balance on the VAT account (output VAT less input VAT) is calculated to establish the amount owed to (or by) HM Revenue & Customs.

VAT is calculated on the **discounted** price, even if the discount is not taken.

Alert. Remember to **round down** the pennies when calculating VAT.

SSAP 5: Sales and purchases shown in the P&L **exclude VAT**.

| Sales and purchase ledgers | Control accounts | VAT | **Errors** | Trial balance |

Journal

The journal records transactions **not covered by other books of original entry**.

The format of a journal entry is:

| Date | Reference | £ | £ |

DEBIT   Account to be debited
CREDIT   Account to be credited

Narrative to explain the transaction

Journals can be used to correct errors. The error **must** have a **debit equal** in value **to the credit**.

Alert. You may be asked for the journal entry of a transaction in an assessment.

Types of error

- Errors of transposition eg writing £381 instead of £318
- Errors of omission eg do not record an invoice
- Errors of principle eg treating capital expense as revenue
- Errors of commission eg recording telephone expenses as electricity costs
- Compensating errors eg telephone costs understated by £342 and electricity cost overstated by £342

| Sales and purchase ledgers | Control accounts | VAT | Errors | **Trial balance** |

Trial balance

A **trial balance** is a list of ledger balances shown in debit and credit columns.

The debits should equal the credits.

If the trial balance does not balance, you need to set up a suspense account.

Suspense account. This is a **temporary** account set up to make the trial balance work. Errors need to be found and corrected, clearing the suspense account, before the final accounts are prepared

Errors not highlighted by trial balance

- **Complete omission** of a transaction
- **Error of commission**: posting to the wrong account
- **Compensating errors**
- **Errors of principle**

3: Introduction to financial statements

Topic List

Equations

Creditors and debtors

Balance sheet

Profit and loss account

Capital and revenue

This chapter deals with the main elements of financial statements. By the end of this Unit, you should be able to prepare a profit and loss account and balance sheet for sole traders and partnerships (see Chapters 10 and 11).

| Equations | Creditors and debtors | Balance sheet | Profit and loss account | Capital and revenue |

What is a business?

A business exists to make a **profit**. Profit is the excess of income over expenditure.

Business equation

$$P = I + D - C$$

P is profit earned in current period

I is increase (or decrease) in net assets in current period

D is drawings in current period

C is capital introduced in current period

Separate entity

A business must always be treated as a separate entity from its owner when preparing accounts.

This derives from the accounting equation: Assets = Capital + Liabilities.

Net assets = total assets less total liabilities

Drawings = capital withdrawn from the business by the owner(s)

Accounting equation

Capital: amount invested in the business by the owner(s). It is owed to the owners(s) and so is a liability.

Accounting equation 1

Assets = Capital + Liabilities

Accounting equation 2

Assets - Liabilities = Capital

Accounting equation 3

Net assets = Capital introduced + retained profits − drawings **or** Retained profit = net assets + drawings − capital introduced

The business equation is then derived from accounting equation 3.

| Equations | **Creditors and debtors** | Balance sheet | Profit and loss account | Capital and revenue |

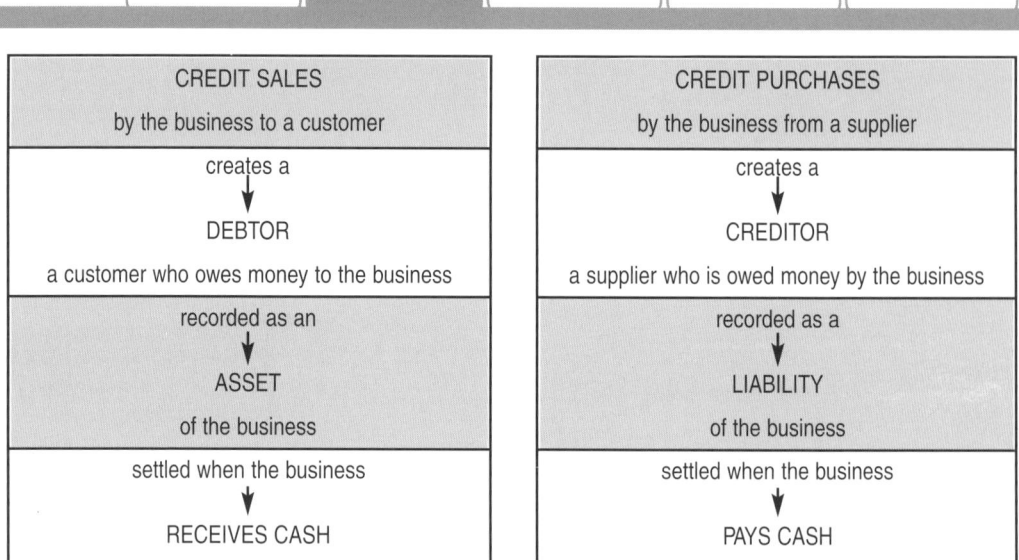

CREDIT SALES	CREDIT PURCHASES
by the business to a customer	by the business from a supplier
creates a	creates a
↓	↓
DEBTOR	CREDITOR
a customer who owes money to the business	a supplier who is owed money by the business
recorded as an	recorded as a
↓	↓
ASSET	LIABILITY
of the business	of the business
settled when the business	settled when the business
↓	↓
RECEIVES CASH	PAYS CASH

| Equations | Creditors and debtors | **Balance sheet** | **Profit and loss account** | Capital and revenue |

Balance sheet

Balance sheet: a statement of the assets, liabilities and capital of a business at a given time

Profit and loss account

Profit and loss account: a statement of revenue earned and costs incurred in earning it

The profit and loss account usually highlights **gross profit** and **net profit**.

The **top part** shows the gross profit for the period.

Gross profit = Sales − Cost of goods sold

The net profit for the period is then calculated.

Net profit = Gross profit + Other income − Other expenses

	Equations	Creditors and debtors	**Balance sheet**	**Profit and loss account**	Capital and revenue

PROFORMA BALANCE SHEET AS AT 31 MARCH 2006

	£	£
Fixed assets		
Land and buildings	X	
Plant and machinery	X	
Fixtures and fittings	<u>X</u>	
		X
Current assets		
Stock	X	
Debtors	X	
Cash at bank and in hand	<u>X</u>	
	<u>A</u>	
Current liabilities		
Trade creditors	X	
Bank overdraft	<u>X</u>	
	<u>B</u>	
Net current assets (A – B)		X
Long-term liabilities		(X)
Net assets		<u>C</u>

Capital
Proprietor's capital X
Retained profits (including previous and current period profits) $\underline{X}$
$\underline{\underline{C}}$

PROFIT AND LOSS ACCOUNT FOR THE PERIOD ENDED 31 MARCH 2006

	£	£
Sales		X
Cost of sales		$\underline{X}$
Gross profit		X
Selling costs	X	
Distribution costs	X	
Administrative expenses	$\underline{X}$	
		$\underline{X}$
Profit retained for the current year		$\underline{\underline{X}}$

| Equations | Creditors and debtors | Balance sheet | Profit and loss account | **Capital and revenue** |

Capital and revenue items

Capital expenditure

Results in the acquisition of fixed assets or an improvement in an existing fixed asset's earning capacity

Revenue expenditure

Expenditure incurred during trading activities or to maintain current earning capacity (ie repairs)

Capital income

Proceeds from the sale of fixed assets

Revenue income

Proceeds from sale of goods or rent, interest and dividends earned from fixed assets

Alert. You must be able to identify, record and account for capital and revenue items accurately.

4: Accounting concepts and standards

Topic List

Accounting concepts

Development of accounting standards

Relevant accounting standards

This chapter deals with the conceptual basis of accounts preparation, the 'why?' as opposed to the 'how?'.

| | Accounting concepts | Development of accounting standards | Relevant accounting standards |

What are accounting concepts?

Accounting concepts are the **assumptions** underlying the financial accounts. Per FRS 18, the most important accounting concepts are **going concern** and **accruals** (or matching).

Going concern

Assumes that the business will continue to operate into the foreseeable future at its current level of activity.

Accruals (matching)

Revenue must be matched against the costs incurred in earning it.

Other concepts

Prudence

Where there is a choice of procedures or valuations, the one selected should give the **most cautious** presentation of the business results.

- Where a loss is foreseen it should be accounted for
- Profit should not be accounted for until it is recognised

Consistency

- Similar items should be given similar treatment
- The same treatment should be applied from one period to another

Materiality

Only material items should appear in the financial statements.

Items are **material** if their omission or misstatement would affect the impact of the financial statements on the reader.

Rule of thumb: items > 5% of net profit.

- Context important
- Some items are 'sensitive'
- Borrowing should not be 'netted off' against cash balances

| | Accounting concepts | Development of accounting standards | Relevant accounting standards |

Development of accounting standards

Accounting standard: a set of rules which prescribe the methods by which accounts should be prepared and presented.

Structure of standard-setting framework:

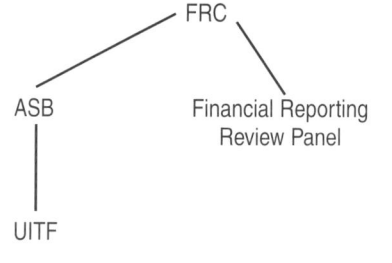

Relevant standards for Unit 5

FRS 15	Tangible fixed assets
FRS 18	Accounting policies
SSAP 5	Accounting for VAT
SSAP 9	Stocks and long-term contracts
SSAP 21	Accounting for leases

Statement of principles

- Relevance
- Reliability
- Comparability
- Understandability

5: Capital expenditure, depreciation and disposals

Topic List

The basics

Acquisitions

Fixed assets register

Depreciation

Disposals

Reconciliation

This is a very important chapter. It covers capital transactions, which you are very likely to come across, both in the workplace and in your exam.

| The basics | Acquisitions | Fixed assets register | Depreciation | Disposals | Reconciliation |

Fixed assets: the basics

Fixed asset: acquired and retained within the business with a view to earning profits, normally used over more than one accounting period.

Generally only **material** assets are capitalised.

Tangible fixed asset

A **physically present** fixed asset:

- Plant and machinery
- Motor vehicles
- Land and buildings

Intangible fixed asset

A fixed asset with **no physical existence**:

- Patent right
- Database
- Trademark

Funding

- Cash
- Borrowing
- Hire purchase
- Leasing
- Part exchange

Step 1	Record inflow of funds.

Step 2	Record outflow of funds and acquisition of the asset.

Authorisation: Any capital expenditure above a certain amount must be authorised; usually a **capital expenditure authorisation form** records this.

Organisational implications

- **Liquidity**. The purchase of a fixed asset may seriously affect cash flow
- **Staffing/training**. A new machine may need skilled operatives
- **Productivity/profitability.** New machinery should improve productivity and profitability
- **Marketing.** Existing customers informed and new customers found in order to fully utilise asset
- **Running expenses**. Most fixed assets require fuel and/or maintenance
- **Premises**. Is there room for more fixed assets?

| The basics | **Acquisitions** | Fixed assets register | Depreciation | Disposals | Reconciliation |

Recording capital acquisitions

The acquisition may be recorded in the **cash book** or in the **purchase day book**.

However, the acquisition is more likely to be recorded with a **journal**.

Journal 1

| 13 Sept 06 DEBIT | Motor vehicles a/c | £13,200 | |
| CREDIT | Spiller Ltd | | £13,200 |

Being purchase of Peugeot 206
LM23 OLE

Journal 2

13 Sept 06 DEBIT	Plant & machinery	£14,000	
DEBIT	VAT	£2,450	
CREDIT	Cash		£16,450

Being purchase of printing machine

| The basics | Acquisitions | **Fixed assets register** | Depreciation | Disposals | Reconciliation |

Fixed assets register

Fixed assets register: listing of all assets owned by the organisation.

- Not part of the double entry
- An internal control

Likely details:
- Description and location of asset
- Purchase date
- Cost
- Depn method and estimated useful life
- Accumulated depn b/f and c/f
- Disposal date and proceeds
- Profit/loss on disposal

| The basics | Acquisitions | Fixed assets register | **Depreciation** | Disposals | Reconciliation |

Depreciation

Depreciation: the measure of the use, wearing out and other fall in useful economic life of a fixed asset.

Depreciation is charged to allocate a fair proportion of the fixed asset's cost to the period benefiting from its use.

Depreciable amount = Cost – Expected residual value

DEBIT ⟶ Profit and loss ⟶ Depn charge for the year
CREDIT ⟶ Balance sheet ⟶ Accumulated depn

Depreciation is **not** a cash expense. Depreciation is **not** an asset replacement fund.

Judgements must be made on:

- Estimated useful life
- Method and rate of depreciation
- Residual value

The consistency concept demands that the same method of depreciation is used year on year.

Methods of depreciation

Straight line

$$\frac{\text{Cost of asset} - \text{residual value}}{\text{Expected useful life of asset}}$$

The depreciation charge is the same year on year.

Reducing balance

n% × The net book value of the asset.

The depreciation charge is higher in the first years of the asset's life.

Alert. Make sure that you learn both methods of depreciation. If you are given details of a fixed asset which is purchased in the middle of the year, remember to adjust the depreciation charge for the months it was not in use during the year.

| The basics | Acquisitions | Fixed assets register | **Depreciation** | Disposals | Reconciliation |

Recording depreciation in the accounts

1 Bring the credit balance of the accumulated depreciation down.

2 Depreciation charge:

DEBIT   Depreciation expense (P&L a/c)
CREDIT   Provision for depreciation a/c (accumulated depreciation)

3 Fixed asset accounts are unchanged, showing the cost of the fixed assets.

Net book value = Fixed asset cost less accumulated depreciation

| The basics | Acquisitions | Fixed assets register | Depreciation | **Disposals** | Reconciliation |

Disposing of fixed assets

	£	£
Sales proceeds		X
Less cost of making the sale		(X)
Net sale proceeds		X
Cost of fixed asset	X	
Less accumulated depreciation	(X)	
Net book value		(X)
Profit/(loss) on disposal		X/(X)

1 Calculate the profit/loss on disposal.

2 The following must appear in the disposals account.
- Original cost of the asset (DR)
- Accumulated depn (CR)
- Net sales proceeds (CR)

| The basics | Acquisitions | Fixed assets register | Depreciation | **Disposals** | Reconciliation |

3. Ledger accounting entries:
   (a) DEBIT   Disposal of fixed asset account
       CREDIT Fixed asset account

       with cost of asset

   (b) DEBIT   Provn for depn a/c
       CREDIT Disposal of fixed asset account

       with accumulated depn

   (c) DEBIT   Debtor account or cash book
       CREDIT Disposal of fixed asset account

       with proceeds of asset sale

4. The balance on the disposal account is the profit/loss which is recorded in the profit and loss account.

DISPOSAL OF FIXED ASSET			
	£		£
Fixed asset a/c	200	Provn for depn a/c	100
Profit and loss a/c		Cash/debtor a/c	130
(profit)	30		
	230		230

Alert. Disposals are a key area. Make sure you can post the ledger entries correctly.

Part exchange

This is an added complication.

The sales proceeds for the disposal is the part exchange value.

DEBIT The new fixed assets account
CREDIT The disposal account
with the part exchange values

Any additional cost of the new asset is accounted for by:

DEBIT The new fixed assets account
CREDIT Cash/creditor
with the balance paid on the new asset

Disposals, like acquisitions, need to be **authorised**.

| The basics | Acquisitions | Fixed assets register | Depreciation | Disposals | Reconciliation |

Reconciling physical assets, ledgers accounts and register

The fixed assets register must reconcile with both the main ledger and the assets themselves.

The cost and accumulated depn totals in the fixed assets register must be compared to the main ledgers.

Discrepancies

Discrepancies have to be investigated.

Items listed in the fixed assets register must be physically inspected on a regular basis.

The fixed assets register must be kept up to date.

Discrepancies need to be followed up.

6: Final accounts and the accounting system

Topic List

Introduction to final accounts

Accounting system

Classifying income and expenditure

Leases

This chapter puts the accounting system into context by means of a diagram. It also introduces ways of classifying income and expenditure.

SSAP 21 on leases is a straightforward standard that may come up as part of a short answer question.

| Introduction to final accounts | **Accounting system** | Classifying income and expenditure | Leases |

Introduction to final accounts

Why prepare accounts?

- To help manage the business
- To calculate key numbers (ie share of profits)
- As a basis of the tax due calculations
- Limited companies must by law

Accounting system

Study the following diagram carefully. You're now in a position to understand all of the elements that make up the accounting system.

Professional behaviour

- Confidentiality
- Tact
- Courtesy

Notes

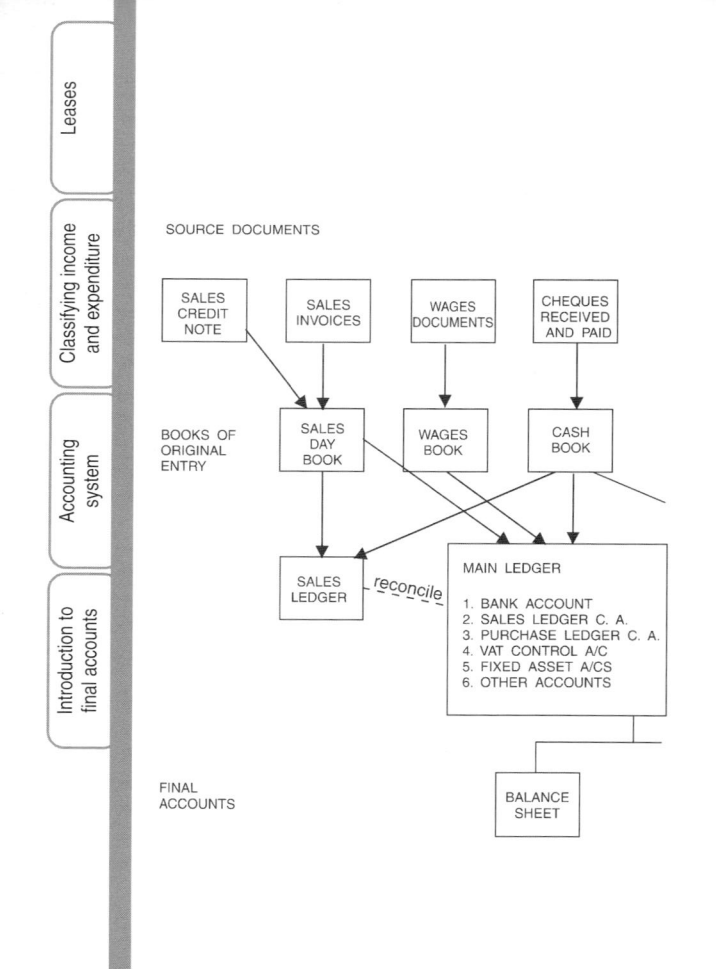

Accounting System Flowchart

Source Documents → Books of Original Entry → Main Ledger → Final Accounts

Source Documents	Books of Original Entry	Main Ledger	Final Accounts
SALES CREDIT NOTE	SALES DAY BOOK	MAIN LEDGER:	BALANCE SHEET
SALES INVOICES	SALES DAY BOOK	1. BANK ACCOUNT	
WAGES DOCUMENTS	WAGES BOOK	2. SALES LEDGER C. A.	
CHEQUES RECEIVED AND PAID	CASH BOOK	3. PURCHASE LEDGER C. A.	
		4. VAT CONTROL A/C	
		5. FIXED ASSET A/CS	
		6. OTHER ACCOUNTS	

SALES DAY BOOK → SALES LEDGER (reconcile with Main Ledger)

Tabs (bottom):
- Introduction to final accounts
- Accounting system
- Classifying income and expenditure
- Leases

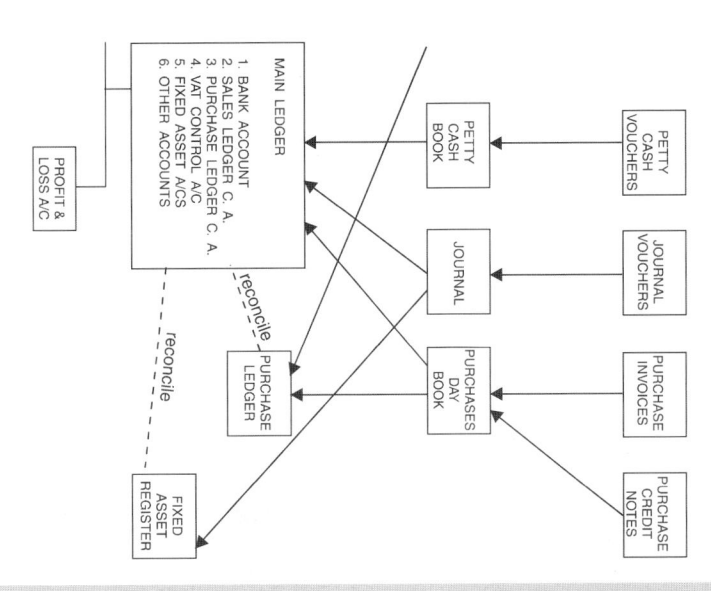

```
PETTY CASH VOUCHERS ──▶ PETTY CASH BOOK ──▶ MAIN LEDGER
                                            1. BANK ACCOUNT
JOURNAL VOUCHERS ──▶ JOURNAL ──────────▶    2. SALES LEDGER C. A.
                                            3. PURCHASE LEDGER C. A.
PURCHASE INVOICES ──▶ PURCHASES DAY ──▶     4. VAT CONTROL A/C
PURCHASE CREDIT NOTES ──▶ BOOK              5. FIXED ASSET A/CS
                                            6. OTHER ACCOUNTS

PURCHASE LEGDER ◀---reconcile--- MAIN LEDGER
FIXED ASSET REGISTER ◀---reconcile--- MAIN LEDGER
PROFIT & LOSS A/C
```

| Introduction to final accounts | Accounting system | **Classifying income and expenditure** | Leases |

Classifying income and expenditure

1 Create accounts for specific items.

2 Guidelines help determine where items are posted. Transactions are posted accordingly.

3 The coding is checked. Queries are referred to a manager.

4 A manager reviews posting summaries.

Profit and loss a/c headings

- Selling and distribution expenses
- Administration expenses
- Finance expenses

| Introduction to final accounts | Accounting system | Classifying income and expenditure | **Leases** |

SSAP 21

Finance lease: transfers substantially all the risks and rewards of ownership to the lessee. → Treated as if the asset has been acquired by the lessee and financed by a loan from the lessor.

Operating lease: any lease that is not a finance lease. → Treated as if it is a rental agreement, with lease payments going through the profit and loss account.

Alert. The standards state that you need to know the difference between operating and finance leases, with an overview of the accounting treatment.

Notes

7: Accruals, prepayments and bad/doubtful debts

Topic List

Matching concept

Accruals and prepayments

Bad and doubtful debts

You've met the concept of accruals before - this chapter tells you how to deal with them in practice.

You also cover the treatment of bad and doubtful debts.

| Matching concept | Accruals and prepayments | Bad and doubtful debts |

Matching concept

Accrual: an unpaid expense charged to the period because it was incurred in the period

Prepayment: a payment made in one period but charged to the later period to which it relates

Accruals

1 Review accruals listing for previous year.

2 Review every income and expenditure account.

3 Review all invoices received after the year end.

4 Calculate the relevant accruals.

| Matching concept | **Accruals and prepayments** | Bad and doubtful debts |

Prepayments

1 Review list of prepayments from previous year.

2 Review all expense accounts for the year.

3 Calculate and list all prepayments.

Payments received in advance (deferred income) are the opposite of prepayments.

Accounting entries

Accruals:

DEBIT Expenses
CREDIT Accruals

Prepayments:

DEBIT Prepayments
CREDIT Expenses

Deferred income:

DEBIT Income
CREDIT Liability

| | | Matching concept | Accruals and prepayments | Bad and doubtful debts |

Types of accrual and prepayment

	£	
Electricity/gas	X ←	Estimate based on previous bills (accrual)
Telephone	X ←	Calls estimate (accrual); rental is prepaid
Rent	X ←	Is rent paid in advance (prepayment) or arrears (accrual)?
Salaries	X ←	One month's accrual if paid in arrears?
Salesperson's expenses	X ←	Specific expense claims (accrual)
Purchases	X ←	Goods received not invoiced (accrual)
	X	

| Matching concept | Accruals and prepayments | **Bad and doubtful debts** |

Bad and doubtful debts

A debtor should only be classed as an asset if it is recoverable.

Bad debts

If definitely irrecoverable, the prudence concept dictates that it should be written off to the profit and loss account as a bad debt.

DEBIT   Bad debts expense (P&L)
CREDIT Sales ledger control

Doubtful debts

If uncertainty exists as to the recoverability of the debt, prudence dictates that a provision should be set up. This is offset against the debtors balance on the balance sheet.

DEBIT   Doubtful debts expense
CREDIT Provision for doubtful debts

Provisions can either be specific, against a particular debtor, or general, against a proportion of all debtors not specifically provided for.

| | Matching concept | Accruals and prepayments | **Bad and doubtful debts** |

When calculating the general provision to be made, the following order applies.

	£
Debtors balance per sales ledger control	X
Less: bad debts written off	(X)
amounts specifically provided	(X)
Balance on which general provision is calculated	X

Note. Only the **movement** in the general provision needs to be accounted for.

	£
Provision required	X
Existing provision	(X)
Increase/(decrease) required	X/(X)

Accounting entries

		DR	CR
(1)	Write off bad debts	Bad debt expense	Sales ledger control
(2)	Write back bad debts when paid in period	Bank or sales ledger control (see below)	Bad debt expense or sundry income
(3)	Set up general provision	Doubtful debts expense	Provision for doubtful debts
(4)	Increase general provision	Doubtful debts expense	Provision for doubtful debts
(5)	Reduce general provision	Provision for doubtful debts	Doubtful debts expense

Subsequent recovery of debts

If a bad debt is recovered, having previously been written off in the period, then:

DEBIT   Sales ledger control
CREDIT Bad debts expense

DEBIT   Cash
CREDIT Sales ledger control

If written off in a previous accounting period, then:

DEBIT   Cash
CREDIT Sundry income

If a doubtful debt previously provided for is recovered, then:

DEBIT   Provision for doubtful debts
CREDIT Doubtful debts expense

DEBIT   Cash
CREDIT Sales ledger control

If a doubtful debt that was provided for in the prior year turns bad, then:

DEBIT   Provision for doubtful debts
CREDIT Sales ledger control

| | Matching concept | Accruals and prepayments | **Bad and doubtful debts** |

VAT bad debt relief

- Six months overdue

- Written off

DEBIT	VAT account (VAT)
DEBIT	Bad debts expense (net)
CREDIT	Sales ledger control (gross)

Alert. Prepayments, accruals and bad and doubtful debts appear in most sittings in both sections of your exam.

8: Stock

Topic List

Cost of goods sold

Accounting for opening and closing stocks

Stocktaking

Valuing stocks

Valuation and profit; SSAP 9

This is an important chapter. It covers stock, which is a key figure in both the profit and loss account and the balance sheet.

You also cover the calculation of cost of goods sold.

| Cost of goods sold | Accounting for opening and closing stocks | Stocktaking | Valuing stocks | Valuation and profit; SSAP 9 |

Formula for the cost of goods sold

	£
Opening stock value	X
Add purchases (or production costs)	X
Carriage inwards	X
	X
Less closing stock value	(X)
Cost of goods sold	X

Carriage inwards

Cost paid by purchaser of having goods transported to his business.

Added to cost of purchases.

Carriage outwards

Cost to the seller, paid by the seller, of having goods transported to customer.

Is a selling and distribution expense, deducted to arrive at net profit.

| Cost of goods sold | **Accounting for opening and closing stocks** | Stocktaking | Valuing stocks | Valuation and profit; SSAP 9 |

Entries during the year

During the year, purchases are recorded by the following entry.

DEBIT   Purchases   £ amount bought
CREDIT   Cash or creditors £ amount bought

The stock account is **not touched at all**.

Entries at year-end

The first thing to do is to transfer the purchases account balance to the profit and loss account:

DEBIT   Profit and loss £ total purchases
CREDIT   Purchases   £ total purchases

The balance on the stock account is still the **opening stock** balance. This must also be transferred to the trading account:

DEBIT   Profit and loss £ opening stock
CREDIT   Stock   £ opening stock

The exact reverse entry is made for the **closing stock (**which will be next year's opening stock):

DEBIT   Stock   £ closing stock
CREDIT   Profit and loss £ closing stock

| Cost of goods sold | Accounting for opening and closing stocks | **Stocktaking** | Valuing stocks | Valuation and profit; SSAP 9 |

Stocktaking

In order to make the entry for the closing stock, we need to know what is in stock at the year-end. We find this out **not** from the accounting records, but by going into the warehouse and actually counting the boxes on the shelves. This is a **stocktake**.

Some businesses keep detailed records of stock coming in and going out, so as not to have to count everything on the last day of the year. These records are **not** part of the double entry system.

| Cost of goods sold | Accounting for opening and closing stocks | Stocktaking | **Valuing stocks** | Valuation and profit; SSAP 9 |

A dealer in, say, kitchen appliances, may know from his stocktake that he has 350 toasters in stock at the year-end. He then needs to know what cash value to place on each toaster. This is the problem of valuation.

Prices

The price used to value an item of stock might be any of a number of possibilities, eg selling price, replacement cost. However, we use the lower of the following.

- The **cost** of buying it
- The **net realisable value** (NRV): the expected selling price less future costs in getting the item ready for sale and selling it

Identification rules

If we are using cost, and units have been bought at different prices during the year, we need to decide which items are left in stock at the year-end.

If the actual cost of each item cannot be used, the possible rules are as follows. Only the first two should be used for financial accounts (as opposed to management accounts).

- FIFO: first in, first out
- AVCO: average cost
- LIFO: last in, first out

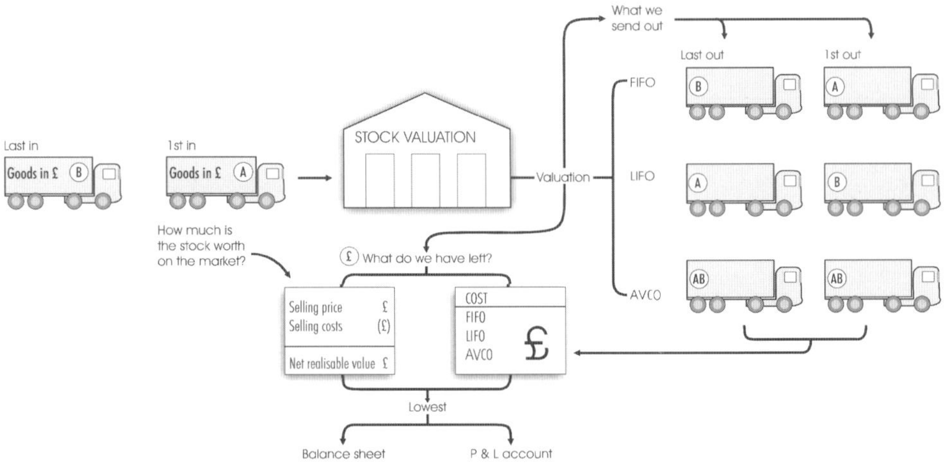

| Cost of goods sold | Accounting for opening and closing stocks | Stocktaking | **Valuing stocks** | Valuation and profit: SSAP 9 |

Stock Valuation

Goods in £ (B) — Last in
Goods in £ (A) — 1st in

What we send out →

FIFO: 1st out (A), Last out (B)
LIFO: 1st out (B), Last out (A)
AVCO: (AB), (AB)

Valuation → What do we have left? £

How much is the stock worth on the market?

COST	£
FIFO	
LIFO	
AVCO	

Net realisable value £
Selling price £
Selling costs (£)

Lowest → Balance sheet, P & L account

| Cost of goods sold | Accounting for opening and closing stocks | Stocktaking | Valuing stocks | **Valuation and profit; SSAP 9** |

Valuation and profit

Different stock valuations produce different cost of sales figures and therefore different profits. This is a temporary difference.

Remember. The higher the closing stock value, the higher the profit.

SSAP 9

- Stock should be valued at the **lower of cost and net realisable value** – the comparison between the two should ideally be made separately for each item
- Cost is the cost incurred in the normal course of business in bringing the product to its present location and condition, including production overheads and some other overheads
- Net realisable value is selling price less costs from now to completion and costs of marketing, selling and distribution
- FIFO and AVCO may be used, but not LIFO

Notes

9: The extended trial balance

Topic List

Purpose

Preparing the ETB

You'll usually get an ETB in your exam and in your simulation test. The only way to master this area is through practice.

| | | Purpose | Preparing the ETB |

Extended trial balance (ETB): a worksheet used to record adjustments between the trial balance and the final accounts

The ETB headings will look something like this.

Ledger account	Trial balance		Adjustments		Profit and loss a/c		Balance sheet	
	Dr £	Cr £	Dr £	Cr £	Dr £	Cr £	Dr £	Cr £

Alert. In some exams you've been required to fill in the adjustments column only and not to extend the trial balance.

	Purpose	Preparing the ETB

Preparing the ETB

1 Draw up the trial balance. Enter it on the ETB and add it up.

2 If debits don't equal credits, check the entries are correct, then insert a suspense account.

3 Make the adjustments required:
- Accruals and prepayments
- Adjustments to stock figures (remember: debit BS with closing stock, credit P&L a/c with closing stock)
- Other adjustments (eg depn and bad debts)

4 Check that the suspense a/c has been cleared by your adjustments.

5 Add the adjustments columns. Check the entries are correct and debits equal credits.

6 Add the figures across each line of the ETB and record total in P&L or balance sheet as appropriate.

7 Add the profit and loss account debit and credits.

	Purpose	Preparing the ETB

8 Take the profit or loss for the period to the balance sheet columns.

- Profit = DEBIT P&L = CREDIT B/S
- Loss = CREDIT P&L = DEBIT B/S

9 Add up the debits and credits in the balance sheet and ensure they are equal. Investigate and resolve any differences.

10: Sole traders

Topic List

Purpose of an ETB

Preparing accounts

Legal status of sole traders

You need to be able to prepare accounts of a sole trader. Tasks usually require preparation of financial accounts from the trial balance or ETB. You must be familiar with this type of question.

	Purpose of an ETB	Preparing accounts	Legal status of sole traders

An extended trial balance essentially records the adjustments which are required to the trial balance in order to produce the final accounts.

Trial balance

List of all balances in the ledger accounts

→

Extended trial balance

Keeps track of adjustments for

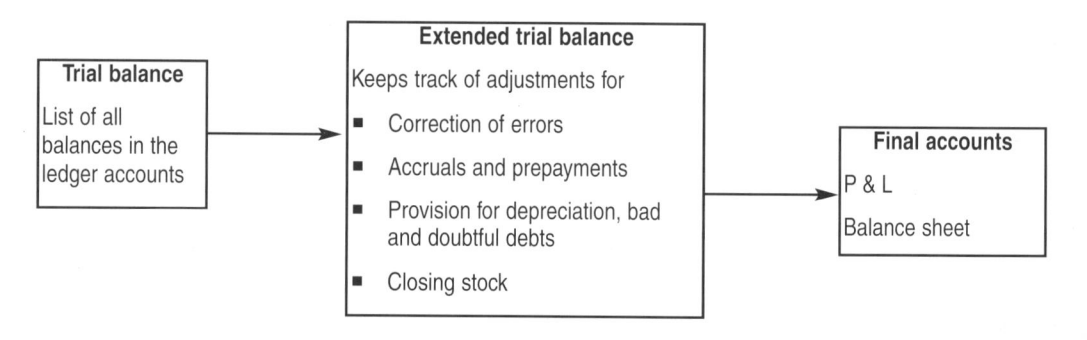

- Correction of errors
- Accruals and prepayments
- Provision for depreciation, bad and doubtful debts
- Closing stock

→

Final accounts

P & L

Balance sheet

The ETB is essentially a worksheet, representing all the ledger account balances and what happens to them.

| Purpose of an ETB | **Preparing accounts** | Legal status of sole traders |

Accounts from the ETB

Ideally it should be a straightforward matter to use the figures in the last two columns of the extended trial balance to draw up the balance sheet and profit and loss account.

However, bear in mind the following points.

- You must know the **format** for a profit and loss account and balance sheet.
- You will need to produce **workings** to get the figures in the ETB into a suitable format

Examples of workings

- Sales and sales returns to be netted off
- Cost of sales working: (opening stock plus purchases (netting off purchase returns) less closing stock)
- Distribution and admin costs, aggregating figures in the ETB
- NBV of all fixed assets for final accounts. Note – total depreciation charge to P&L
- Debtors – need to add in prepayments and take off any provision
- Creditors – need to add in accruals

Alert. Some of these workings, eg cost of sales, can be shown on the face of the P&L or balance sheet. Others may need to be shown separately. Use your judgement as to how complicated the working is likely to be.

Purpose of an ETB	Preparing accounts	Legal status of sole traders

In an exam, you will invariably have to deal with some **post ETB adjustments**. These will be set out in the form of **journal entries**. Here are the ones that are likely to come up most often.

Accrued accountancy fees

The accountant estimates that a further £330 needs to be accrued for finalising the accounts.

DEBIT	Accountancy	£330	
CREDIT	Accruals		£330

Drawings, not wages

The owner realises that £500 in the wages account was actually drawn by her, not paid to a staff member.

DEBIT	Drawings	£500	
CREDIT	Wages		£500

Bank charges

The bank sends a letter stating that interest of £170 and charges of £138 were accrued at the year end.

DEBIT	Bank interest	£170	
	Bank charges	£138	
CREDIT	Accruals		£308

Write-off of a bad debt

A customer has gone bankrupt owing £5,000.

DEBIT	Bad debt expense	£5,000	
CREDIT	Sales ledger control		£5,000

Alert. Learn the above entries by heart! Then practise, practise, practise!

You will normally be asked to do the journal entries **before** producing the final accounts.

Remember to take account of these adjustments, as well as the information on the ETB, in preparing your final accounts. For instance:

- Your creditors figure may now include accountancy and bank interest accruals
- Your debtors may be less and your P&L bad debt expense will need to be increased

Accounts from other sources

The standards show that you may be required to draft sole trader accounts from sources other than the ETB.

- Write up the ledger accounts, extract a trial balance and include final adjustments
- Given a trial balance and a list of items to be adjusted
- A trial balance may include a suspense account to be cleared

Purpose of an ETB	Preparing accounts	Legal status of sole traders

The sole trader is liable for **all** the liabilities of a business to the extent of his or her personal wealth.

Contrast with limited companies: shareholders' liability is limited to the extent of their shareholding in the company.

Advantages of sole traders	Disadvantages
■ Fewer rules to follow	■ Unlimited liability
■ Only simplified accounts	■ Harder to raise capital
■ No audit	
■ No supervision from registrar or DTI	

11: Partnerships

Topic List

Characteristics

Preparing partnership accounts

Retirement or death of a partner

Admission of a new partner

Partnership accounts have a lot in common with sole trader accounts. However, there are differences in the way profit is appropriated and the way capital is presented in the balance sheet.

| Characteristics | Preparing partnership a/cs | Retirement or death of a partner | Admission of a new partner |

Definition: A partnership is an arrangement between two or more individuals in which they undertake to share the risks and rewards of a joint business operation.

Partnership agreement	No partnership agreement
There is usually a partnership agreement setting out the financial arrangements, eg:	Partnership Act 1890 applies.

Partnership agreement

There is usually a partnership agreement setting out the financial arrangements, eg:

- The amount of capital to be provided by each partner

- The division of profits between partners. Profits might be earned in the form of salaries, interest on capital and residual profit share. The agreement will usually specify a ratio (the profit sharing ratio) in which residual profits are to be shared by the partners

No partnership agreement

Partnership Act 1890 applies.

- Residual profits are shared equally between the partners

- There are no partners' salaries

- Partners receive no interest on the capital they invest in the business

- Partners are entitled to interest of 5% per annum on any loans they advance to the business in excess of their agreed capital

Advantages and disadvantages

Partnership v sole trader

Advantages

- Spread risk
- Network of contacts
- Partners bring in business, skills and experience
- Easier to raise finance

Disadvantages

- Profits spread
- Dilution of control
- Disputes between partners

Partnership v limited company

Advantages

- No need to comply with statutory requirements such as audit
- No need to comply with accounting standards
- No formation or registration fees

Disadvantage

- No limited liability

		Characteristics		Preparing partnership a/cs	Retirement or death of a partner	Admission of a new partner

Capital and current accounts

It is usual to maintain both a capital account and a current account for each partner.

A partner's capital account shows any cash or other assets brought by him into the business. He will usually make an initial capital contribution when he joins the partnership, but there may also be further injections (or withdrawals) of capital later on.

While the balance on a partner's capital account is likely to remain stable for long periods, his current account balance will fluctuate more rapidly.

PROFORMA CURRENT ACCOUNT

	X £	Y £	Z £		X £	Y £	Z £
Drawings	X	X	X	Balance b/f	X	X	X
				Salary	X	X	X
				Interest on capital	X	X	X
Balance c/f	X	X	X	Profit share	X	X	X
	X	X	X		X	X	X

Appropriation accounts

After calculating the net profit earned by the business an appropriation account must be prepared to determine the allocation of profit between the partners.

The sum available for appropriation must be shared amongst the partners and credited to their current accounts.

- Some partners may be entitled to a salary. This is credited to the partner concerned and taken out of the 'pool' available for appropriation

- Partners may be entitled to interest on their capital account balances. Each partner is credited with the appropriate amount and again the 'pool' is reduced

- Finally, the residual 'pool' of profits is shared amongst the partners in their profit sharing ratio

| Characteristics | **Preparing partnership a/cs** | Retirement or death of a partner | Admission of a new partner |

PROFORMA APPROPRIATION ACCOUNT

	£	£
Net profit		X
Less: salary: A	X	
interest on capital: A	X	
B	X	
C	X	(X)
Profit		X

		£	£
Appropriation:	A	X	
	B	X	
	C	X	
			X

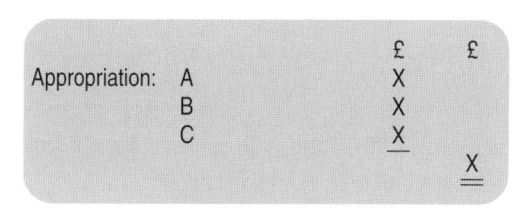

When a partner makes a loan to the partnership he is a creditor of the partnership. The loan is shown separately from the partner's capital as a long-term liability.

Remember:

- Interest on a partner's loan is a P&L expense not an appropriation.
- If no interest rate is specified, the rate is 5% (following the Partnership Act)

| Characteristics | Preparing partnership a/cs | **Retirement or death of a partner** | Admission of a new partner |

Retirement or death of a partner

1 Prepare the profit and loss account

2 Split profit between pre-change and post-change periods, on the following basis.
- Gross profit: based on turnover (take care over seasonal variations in turnover)
- Specific expenses: charge to appropriate period (eg bad debts - relates to period in which sale was made)
- Other expenses: on a time basis

3 Pre-change profit
- Appropriate salary, interest and profit share using **old** partnership agreement
- Put old partners' drawings through current account

4 Balance off retiring partner's **current** account **only**, and transfer the balance to his **capital** account

Calculate goodwill

5
- Credit **old** partners in old PSR in their capital accounts
- This will provide the retiring partner with an increase in the partnership's worth that has arisen while he was a partner

6 Remove the **old** partner; usually the question will give instructions, eg:
- Pay in cash (DR Capital a/c; CR Cash)
- Create a loan account (DR Capital a/c; CR Loan)

7 Write off the goodwill by debiting all the remaining partners in the **new** PSR

8 Balance off the capital accounts, and then calculate any interest on capital (according to the **new** agreement) on the **new** capital balances

9 Post-change profit
- Deduct any interest owed to retired partner
- Appropriate remainder using **new** partnership agreement re salary, interest and profit share

10 Prepare the balance sheet if required to do so

Alert. So far exam questions have usually asked for an appropriation account and capital and current accounts. Admission or retirement are tested, involving goodwill. Goodwill is usually eliminated from the books.

| Characteristics | Preparing partnership a/cs | Retirement or death of a partner | **Admission of a new partner** |

Admission

1 Prepare the profit and loss account

2 Split between pre-change and post-change periods, on the following basis.
   - Gross profit: based on turnover (take care over seasonal variations in turnover)
   - Specific expenses: charge to appropriate period (eg bad debts - relates to period in which sale was made)
   - Other expenses: on a time basis

3 Pre-change profit
   - Appropriate salary, interest and profit share using **old** partnership agreement
   - Allow an extra column for new partner, in both current and capital accounts

4 Calculate goodwill
   - Credit **old** partners in old PSR in their capital accounts

5 Write off the goodwill by debiting all the partners (ie include the newly admitted partner) in the **new** PSR

6 Balance off the capital accounts, and then calculate any interest on capital (according to the **new** agreement) on the **new** capital balances

7 Post-change profit
- Appropriate remainder using **new** partnership agreement re salary, interest and profit share

8 Put drawings through the current accounts

9 Prepare the balance sheet if required to do so

> **Alert.** The examiner has indicated that a question will deal with either a retirement or an admission, but not both in the same question.

Change in partnership agreement

If partners all continue through the period, but change the profit sharing ratio during the period, profit must be split in the appropriation account between the pre- and the post-change period, and must then be appropriated differently for each period re salary, interest and profit share.

Notes

12: Incomplete records

Topic List

Opening balance sheet

Credit sales, purchases and cost of sales

Stolen or destroyed goods

Cash book

Accruals, prepayments and drawings

This area is a very good test of your accounts preparation knowledge.

You need to know how the accounts fit together in order to fill in the blanks.

| Opening balance sheet | Credit sales, purchases and cost of sales | Stolen or destroyed goods | Cash book | Accruals, prepayments and drawings |

Types of question

An incomplete records question may require competence in dealing with one or more of the following.

- Preparation of accounts from information in the question
- Theft of cash (balance on the cash in hand account is unknown)
- Theft or destruction of stock (closing stock is the unknown)
- Estimated figures, eg 'drawings are between £15 and £20 per week'
- Calculation of capital by means of net assets
- Calculation of profit by P = increase in net assets plus drawings minus increase in capital
- Calculation of year end stock when the stocktake was done after the year end

Opening balance sheet

Often a task provides information about the assets and liabilities of a business at the beginning of a period, leaving you to calculate capital as the balancing figure.

Remember

Assets – liabilities = Proprietor's capital

| Opening balance sheet | **Credit sales, purchases and cost of sales** | Stolen or destroyed goods | Cash book | Accruals, prepayments and drawings |

Credit sales and debtors

The key lies in the formula linking sales, cash receipts and debtors.

Remember

Opening debtors + sales − cash receipts = closing debtors

Alternatively put all the workings into a control account to calculate the figure you want.

Purchases and trade creditors

Similarly you need a formula for linking purchases, cash payments and creditors.

Opening creditors + purchases − cash payments
= closing creditors

Use a control account.

SALES LEDGER CONTROL ACCOUNT

	£		£
Opening debtors	X	Cash receipts	X
Sales	X	Closing debtors	X
	X		X

PURCHASE LEDGER CONTROL ACCOUNT

	£		£
Cash payments	X	Opening creditors	X
Closing creditors	X	Purchases	X
	X		X

| | | | Opening balance sheet | | **Credit sales, purchases and cost of sales** | | Stolen or destroyed goods | | Cash book | | Accruals, prepayments and drawings | |

Gross margins and mark ups

Other incomplete records problems revolve around the relationship between sales, cost of sales and gross profit: in other words, they are based on reconstructing a trading account. Bear in mind the crucial formula.

		%
	Cost of sales	100
Plus	Gross profit	25
Equals	Sales	125

Gross profit may be expressed either as a percentage of cost of sales or as a percentage of sales.

- In the example, gross profit is 25% of cost of sales (ie 25/100). The terminology is a 25% **mark up**

- Gross profit can also be expressed as 20% of sales (ie 25/125). The terminology is a 20% gross margin or **gross profit percentage**. The proforma would appear as follows

		%
	Cost of sales	80
Plus	Gross profit	20
Equals	Sales	100

| Opening balance sheet | Credit sales, purchases and cost of sales | **Stolen or destroyed goods** | Cash book | Accruals, prepayments and drawings |

Stolen goods or goods destroyed

The cost of goods stolen/destroyed can be calculated as follows.

	£
Cost of goods sold based on gross profit margin or mark up	A
Cost of goods sold calculated using standard formula (ie opening stock plus purchases less closing stock)	(B)
Difference (lost/stolen stock)	C

- If no goods have been lost, A and B should be the same and therefore C should be nil

- If goods have been lost, B will be larger than A, because some goods which have been purchased were neither sold nor remaining in stock, ie they have been lost

- Stolen or lost stock is accounted for in two ways depending on whether the goods were insured

If insured		If not insured	
DEBIT	Insurance claim (debtor)	DEBIT	Expenses
CREDIT	Purchases	CREDIT	Purchases

| Opening balance sheet | Credit sales, purchases and cost of sales | Stolen or destroyed goods | **Cash book** | Accruals, prepayments and drawings |

Cash book

Incomplete records problems often concern small retail businesses where sales are mainly for cash. A two-column cash book is often the key to preparing final accounts.

- The bank column records cheques drawn on the business bank account and cheques received from customers and other sources
- The cash column records till receipts and any expenses or drawings paid out of till receipts before banking

Debits (receipts)		Credits (payments)	
Cash	Bank	Cash	Bank
£	£	£	£

Don't forget that movements between cash and bank need to be recorded by contra entries. This will usually be cash receipts lodged in the bank (debit bank column, credit cash column), but could also be withdrawals of cash from the bank to top up the till (debit cash column, credit bank column).

Again, incomplete records problems will often feature an unknown figure to be derived. Enter in the credit of the cash column all amounts known to have been paid from till receipts: expenses, drawings, lodgements into bank. Enter in the debit of the cash column all receipts from cash customers or other cash sources.

- The balancing figure may then be a large debit, representing the value of cash sales if that is the unknown figure
- Alternatively it may be a credit entry that is needed to balance, representing the amount of cash drawings or of cash stolen

| Opening balance sheet | Credit sales, purchases and cost of sales | Stolen or destroyed goods | Cash book | **Accruals, prepayments and drawings** |

Accruals and prepayments

When there is an accrued expense or prepayment, the P & L charge can be calculated from the opening balance, the cash movement and the closing balance.

Sometimes it helps to use a 'T' account, eg as follows (for a rent payment).

RENT

	£		£
Prepayment: bal b/f	700	P & L a/c (bal fig)	9,000
Cash	9,300	Prepayment: bal c/f	1,000
	10,000		10,000

Drawings

Note three tricky points about drawings.

- Owner pays personal income into business bank account

    DEBIT   Cash
    CREDIT Drawings

- Owner pays personal expenses out of business bank account

    DEBIT   Drawings
    CREDIT Cash

- Wording of an exam question

    - 'Drawings approximately £40 per week'
      ∴ Drawings for year = £40 × 52 = £2,080

    - 'Drawings between £35 and £45 per week'
      ∴ Drawings are a missing number to be calculated

| Opening balance sheet | Credit sales, purchases and cost of sales | Stolen or destroyed goods | Cash book | **Accruals, prepayments and drawings** |

Incomplete records and your exam

- **Most past exams** have contained an incomplete records element

- Your incomplete records task will be **broken down** into several sub-tasks. In other words, you won't have to prepare the trading account from scratch but will get there step by step